Jean Atkin

High Nowhere

Indigo Dreams Publishing

First Edition: High Nowhere
First published in Great Britain in 2023 by:
Indigo Dreams Publishing Ltd
24 Forest Houses
Halwill
Beaworthy
EX21 5UU
www.indigodreamspublishing.com

Jean Atkin has asserted her right under the Copyright, Designs
and Patents Act 1988 to be identified as the author of this work.
© 2023 Jean Atkin

ISBN 978-1-912876-80-8

British Library Cataloguing in Publication Data. A CIP record
for this book can be obtained from the British Library.

Designed and typeset in Palatino Linotype by Indigo Dreams.
Cover design by Ronnie Goodyer
All photographs © 2023 Jean Atkin
Printed and bound in Great Britain by 4edge Ltd.

Papers used by Indigo Dreams are recyclable products made
from wood grown in sustainable forests following the guidance
of the Forest Stewardship Council.

To my wonderful sons, Lenny and Dougie, with love,
and hope for the future.

CONTENTS

PATH

High Nowhere

'There are no sacred and unsacred places; there are only sacred and desecrated places.'

~ Wendell Berry

'I think that by retaining one's childhood love of such things as trees, fishes, butterflies and – to return to my first instance – toads, one makes a peaceful and decent future a little more probable, and that by preaching the doctrine that nothing is to be admired except steel and concrete, one merely makes it a little surer that human beings will have no outlet for their surplus energy except in hatred and leader worship.'
George Orwell *Some Thoughts on the Common Toad*

'The sky has not fallen. Not yet.'

~ Donna Haraway

'I'll sing to you to this soft lute, and show you all alive
The World, where every particle of dust breathes forth its joy.'

~ William Blake

BRINK

wood   In High Nowhere now the chiffchaff calls,
sap leaps and our red soil leans into south.

A din of rooks descends the air to strut
as black as beetles. The tatty wood lets out

its rusted ghost of parish tip, ramshackles
down a bank. Wild garlic leafs to cover it.

Ferme d'Isson

It's early among the tents, the bright air
full of dancing flies.
Through the unzipped awning
a cuckoo calls in Brittany
from every wood
cou-cou   cou-cou

its leafy echo louder, even
than the crickets
and straight away
another cuckoo
from another wood
replies

and sunshine pours
on us, our pale skin
cries, yes, yes.
And campers pass, with
washing up in plastic bowls.

By my bare foot, small spiders
web each blade of grass
meanwhile I
shade my eyes
and wonder where
cuck-oo   cuck-oo
have England's cuckoos gone?

1937, Tasmanian Tiger

that long and jagged jaw incised
into cave walls, this creature
stalking out of the Ice Age, drawing
down its stiff striped tail behind it

*(1935) '… a dangerous opponent
now very rare, being forced out
of its habitat by the march of
civilisation…'*

Benjamin's eyes are dark,
unreadable in the twenty
seconds of rescued
film reel. Caged and jerky
she paces fence to fence.

There is a cracked concrete floor.
There is a keeper rattling at the mesh.
She has eighteen months to live.
Benjamin will be the first endling.

In a new century, in a new art
her rounded ears will be
veined leaves
her body once more red and ochre.
Below her tail the dangling

paw of her pouched cub.
The artist has striped and
spotted her coat, dotted it
with all the jewels

of colour that no-one
is going to see again.

The like being not in the world

We don't remember the dodo
was called *fat arse* by Dutch sailors,
or that it fed its chicks on crop-milk
and could live for twenty years.

We don't remember the dodo's visage
was thought melancholy.
Or that it was ridiculed for being
unafraid of humans.

We don't remember the last dodo
in captivity, shipped in 1647
from Mauritius to Nagasaki.
It arrived alive and was considered equal
in value to a white deer and a bezoar.

Remember instead Emmanuel Altham, who sailed
to Mauritius in 1628 and wrote home:
Right wo and loving brother, here are some
very strange fowles, called by ye portingalls, Dodo.
Which for the rareness of the same,
the like being not in the world but here
I have sent you one by Mr Perce
who did arrive with the ship
at this island ye 10th of June.

And in the margin added:
Of Mr Perce you shall receive a jarr of ginger
for my sister, some beades for my cousins,
your daughters, and the bird called a Dodo,
if it live.

1914, Passenger Pigeon
After John Audubon, witness

Pigeons have been killed in the neighbourhood of New York
with their crops full of rice, which they collected
in the fields of Georgia and Carolina.
I have observed them keep high in the air, to survey
hundreds of acres at once. And when the trees are
abundantly hung with mast, they fly low.

Passing over the Barrens in the autumn of 1813
I saw the Pigeons flying, and feeling the inclination
to count the flocks that might pass within the reach of my eye
in one hour, I dismounted, and began to mark with my pencil,
making
a dot for each flock that passed. This proved
impracticable
                        the air was filled with Pigeons; the light of
noon obscured
as if by an eclipse. Their dung fell in spots, not
unlike melting flakes of snow
                        the buzz of wings had lulled my senses to
repose
when a Hawk pressed upon the rear of a flock
                        and at once, like a torrent, like thunder, they
rushed
to a mass, they darted forward in undulating
lines, swept close over the earth
                        with inconceivable speed they
mounted once more as a column, and at height they wheeled
like the coils of a gigantic serpent

On the banks of the Ohio were crowds of men and boys.
They shot constantly at the pilgrims, which flew lower
as they passed the river. Multitudes were destroyed.
For a week, the population talked only of Pigeons
and ate only Pigeons.

On the Barrens, each passes like a thought, and on trying
to see it again, the eye searches in vain;
the bird is gone.

Ode to the Cryptic Treehunter

O little bird of the midstorey, bird of the canopy,
of the bright flowers, of the tall humid trees.
You were long of bill, neat-framed, cinnamon-brown

and screeching. Forager inside the rare and glowing hearts
of arboreal bromeliads. You were wholly new, as the century
began, a species named for being so hard to see, and even then

worn slight as a ghost in the razed forest, your habitats
islanded by fire and blade and plough and profit.
In Portuguese, you were *gritador-do-nordeste*, Screamer

of the Northeast. And though you've gone, it's weird
that we're just clicks away: the internet re-animates you,
screeching from your bulldozed branches

…a bee buzzes close to the mic. Through drumming rain
and audible soft layers of air, you shriek again.
Behind you, bright flares of birdsong rise higher, last for longer…

We blinked, you vanished, in the disappearing trees.
In twenty nineteen, you were classified extinct. We
found you, named you, lost you, in less than twenty years.

Naming the dead

Martha was the last passenger pigeon
Benjamin, the last thylacine
Celia the last Pyrenean ibex
Turgi the last Polynesian tree snail
Xiangxiang, the last Yangtze giant softshell turtle

Lonesome George was the last Pinta Island tortoise
Incas, the last Carolina parakeet
Sudan, the last male white rhino
and Booming Ben, the last heath hen

listen

during that first wave of Covid-19, the deep
oceans quieted
by one point five decibels at
sixty kilometres from shipping lanes

and a marine acoustician said
we have an opportunity to listen

the seismic mapping ships
anchored for a while, paused
in their lawnmower-crawl of the oceans

they stopped drawing three-
dimensional maps of oil
and gas for the shareholders

they did not blast stripes
of pressurised air from guns
into the sea bed, every
ten seconds, around the clock

they did not hit the seabed in soundwaves
penetrate it miles deep, bounce their echo back
to the surface to be
measured with hydrophones

around each air gun is an absence of life

two thirds of zooplankton die
within three quarters of a mile around
each blast

zooplankton feed the molluscs
shrimp and krill
zooplankton are food for sardines
herring, and whales

the whales sing, then stop
for the noise of each container ship
then sing again

but fewer of them
now

to roar and boom and sigh
to fill dark oceans
their voices clicking through their nasal passages

they listen like an eye
changes focus, bounce off distance
and difference

some whales make sounds too low
for us to hear

we can't hear them and they
can't hear each other

the marine acoustician said
we had an opportunity to listen

The birds fly from us

The little birds weighed nothing, made just a whirring
in my head. They split my heart like a seed.
Lifted me to the canopy of trees. My boots left earth.
I tasted leaves. Featherwise, my fingers stretched.

Up there my ears ran wild with calls as fledgling
long-tail tits sang sibling to sibling, those nest-mates
fluttering in acts of grace and clumsiness.
They were a clan, they held me in their space

and hop-flew round me where I hovered between birches.
Bird whirled past bird until one paused and eyed me.
And I saw, as if I'd known it long before, its tiny, downy,
beating heart, like a green ash fire in its side.

Oh how that fledgling teetered, balanced on its long latch tail.
It was midday, and June, and small leaves blew.
The bird still did not know what I was.
Then I breathed out ruin, and on that breath, it flew.

light In High Nowhere now a magpie lies
crisped among blackberries, dark claws clenched.

Its empty eye is clean and full of sun.
Its dulling feathers dredged with dander.

I lift it off the path, see all its layers of light,
hollowed melanosomes left to glitter in the hedge.

SPREAD

clocks   In High Nowhere now they buy hot pies
and zip their coats. The veg stall tips its rain.

A bloke lays out greengrocers' grass. The cauliflowers
are stacked like clouds. The till rings true.

Behind the socially distanced queue blow dandelion
clocks. There goes a thrush, a bus, the cautious crowds.

Yewei

Behind high blue walls, the market at Wuhan
has been closed since January. *Look through the gate,*
he says. There's an arched roof, a fish net, a red bucket.
There's a torn poster for fresh, live Wuchang bream.

Here thousands of penned wild animals were stacked
in cages, sold alive. Thirty-eight different species, wild
and tamed, that never mix in the world outside. Here
they exchanged their pathogens, a viral melting pot.

Stall 29 alone gave up five positive samples, four of them from
wild taste trade. From a metal cage. From a machine to remove
fur, or feathers. From two handcarts for wheeling crates
of creatures in and out, for banquets, snacks, or pets.

lockdown heron

over our postage stamp garden
churning the early air
between roofs I saw a whole

huge heron bank over
the neighbour's ridgepole
and side-slip drop to draw
with grey-sky-elbowed wings
a ragged loop above our pond

with one lean eye it logged
our water   then see-sawed up
each slow wingbeat ferried it
away by the width of each street

I watched it out of sight but
it's hanging in mid-mind
mid-air

isolate   slant   two metres up
above our pond   not twice
two metres
from where I stand

Essential exercise

In this sunnier, odder spring with louder
birdsong, sweeter lanes and tall
blue skies unstreaked by planes

the bicycle carries me with all
its old swiftness, answers the ask
of a leaned corner, flicks its jink around a grid.

For one hour in each slow day I've been
out cycling quiet roundabouts, freewheeling
down these potholed weeks of death.

I've been waving to more cyclists now
than cars. Though once, there was a bin lorry,
and I lapped it, felt my lungs at work.

Thursday, and a swallow skims a fence,
gauges precisely its distance from my wheels.
Ambulances pass. Key workers work and set

aside their fears. They labour through this spring's
long hours, high rent, low pay – the poverty trap.
At eight o'clock, on our doorsteps, we'll all clap.

The hills in lockdown

Wind bends the nettles and I
turn the phone cam on myself
to watch rain gutter off my hood
and down my nose

hair drenched to points
sticks to one cheek
I look in my eyes to see
doubt, of course

while cracked earth gulps all
the droplets sky
shakes loose and a wet bee
crawls in the cave of a foxglove

I breathe wet soil, wet
grass and also, faintly,
something dead. A sign
handwritten, badly spelt

on the farmyard gate, to ask me
not to walk the path just now
seems deeply lonely. Rain,
while I'm outside, is company.

Earth's viral load

To understand viruses, consider
how humans infest the earth.
How each one wants only to live.

SOURCE

A wish on the Glynch

1 Wheel and wallower

The flat leat is a mirror for sky
laid quiet all along to the launder
till the miller leans on his lever
and the penstock frees the flow

Just so below deck the wooden
buckets fill and overtop
and wheel's throat roars
wet speed gets up, and all

three decks of the building thunder
to the mill wheel's diamond spin
its rangy, walled-in stride

Now the crown wheel winks and glances
and in furbelows of cobwebs, how
the wallower dances

2 The rule

Then the miller runs his broad finger
down the master furrow, down
the journeyman furrow
so lightly over
the prentice furrow and the fly

and grain flows into the millstone's eye
cool air exhales
along the gulleys as they grind
and in a single rumbling hour
they fill the mill with scents of bread

and the miller's arms are furred with flour
he rubs it through his fingers as it falls
testing it for any lack, applying
the miller's rule of thumb
above the open sack

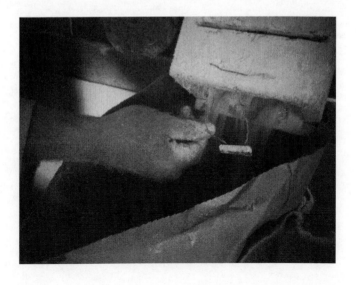

3 The flour dresser machine

And then – they loose the bolter
whose hoofbeats rise, accelerate
beat hard ground in through the ear
the whole mill quakes, dust lifts –

now it's belts to the bolter
at a tearing gallop
and sift of flour through cloth
the bolter lost to sense or safety

and bit between the teeth
– where fear is a source of power –
how the sack fills, and all the air
white-blind with flour

4 A wish on the Glynch

Wish for water
say Clenchers mill and Pepper mill
wish for water, say Berry, Blackford, Staunton mills,
all in a row. Gone are the little mills, like corn
bent under gales, laid low.

Wish for water
sing the birds, through the roof
wish for water, says the miller
setting his three-decked ship to wallow
the leat, and steer the Glynch's tow.

Wish for water
say the millstones, wish for the grain's flow
wish for bread, says the village
bread and summer sunshine, bread and ordinary snow
bread ground for us by the Glynch brook minnow!

Two Stroke, from 1919

The Lister Junior smokes on the beat, belts
spinning easy. Your red metal petrol can

is canted over in the grass, raw clash
with green inside this fumy breeze –

I think air rumbles in your ears
from long ago, this ordinary familiar –

suck, squeeze, bang, blow –
an engine designed in a frugal decade

that freewheels without firing. You
show me how it slows

how governor weights drop in,
valve sucks, fuel flows and

bang –

that rhythmic cough – and off
it goes again –

Death of an oil rig

1

Winner: as if Trafalgar Square were raised on orange castle keeps
and sailing, her derrick doffing like a hat through screaming gulls
that soar above her helipad, that salt-white H out riding on the sea.

Here at the butt of life, condemned at thirty-three and bound
for scrap, she radioes from Stavanger. After that, they switch it off.
They tow her – it will be Malta next, then east.

The tugboat hauls her north into a forecast storm. In darkness
Winner bolts and jibs, her metal skirts make sails before the wind.
She drags her tugboat and at 4am, the towline snaps – she's free.

First light brings her in with the tide, hitched drunk to rocks
off Lewis. Her pontoons scrape the threshing shallows.
She towers over the lean cold fang of the cliff

snags a crosswise strut of chipped and rusting steel – and she locks
to the headland with a crack that sends the seabirds clattering
upwards, and stirs the newly dead below their kirkyard stones.

First residents arrive at dawn with the police. The salvage teams
are got on board. They slither on a pontoon's whaleback – make
a noisy, spray-filled, gasping climb on ropes – this trip so arduous

they opt for days aboard, and sleep in tilted cabins, propping
torn-off doors to make up level beds above the sea.
Three weeks later *Winner's* towed away, and a shuttle bus brings

onlooker islanders in shifts. There's a volunteer-run tea stall.
At 9pm the sun goes down behind the rig and the crowd
slaps midges, snaps photos. Towlines tauten.

And *Winner* inch by inch comes off the rocks. There's clapping.
Tugs tow her north across the bay, still listing, to more applause
as finally she clears a distant headland and is on her way.

2

Hawk, the heavy-lifting ship, sinks herself into the sea, drifts
below the rig and rises. And so *Winner* is lifted out of Scotland.
They steal away in darkness, going south.

They sail for the Alboran Sea. *Winner* is worth zero dollars per ton
in Europe but big bucks in the east. The further east
the better price (the more shipbreaker deaths).

From his Valletta rooftop, a retired professor trains binoculars.
Then rides his motorbike down to the coast. *Hawk and Winner*
he tells his wife later, *a couple, but a very temporary affair.*

Hawk batters on through the Aegean, east for Aliaga –
because this is responsible disposal, the price far less
than in the breakers' yards of Chittagong and Alang.

Winner sails under her own name, has nothing to hide.
At Aliaga, the shore's on fire. Blowtorches rip through hulls,
a frigate's haloed, a cargo carrier sparks long rusty fountains.

The foreman boards the rig. They wrap thick chains round each
of *Winner*'s orange legs. The links weigh slowly back to land.
Four chains fly taut above the waves as bulldozers start up.

They drag the thrashing rig through shallows up the beach
a lurching, fighting fish that bucks and groans. In fires
and shrieking steel they beach her by a halved Del Monte ship.

In a swinging cage, the blowtorch crew is slung to deck.
They target the helipad because it's at the top – shipbreakers
burn downwards. They use *Winner*'s own cranes to yank it away.

In a fortnight just the horizontal decks remain. Also a leather logbook
filled with lost decades' names of all of those who worked
their watch on *Winner*. Their signatures are neat, and for the flames.

With the millers of air

Look up at them, their rotor cones revolve the flying sky.
Learn them – long gods of the upper air, they oil
their mesmer so we watch   and watch   and watch
blades pale as wings, angelic almost, chop the firmament.

Up there they borrow and re-make its power. Each gleans
the air for tangential spin. Electrons dance magnetic fields
to pass and re-pass coppered coils. They cannot tire.
They reap as long as the wind can blow.

Know them, who range above cattle and bog cotton on Blackcraig.
Who wade the liminal, high ghosts of the Solway sandbanks.
Who flicker in and out of salt, heads fogged,
their work a thresh of certainty and doubt.

Jockeyed by their wild anemometers, they turn
their faces windward, will race night and day
for twenty years. Here gallop the millers of air,
grinding the winds of nowhere.

slick   In High Nowhere now we work a wheel
to level the hill and pound the field.

We work the phones in shifts. They contract out,
and dirty money turns its trick.

Bright plastics roam our bloodstreams and our seas.
The price of oil is everywhere, and slick.

HIGH NOWHERE

north   In High Nowhere now there's altitude.
I am reduced to trudge and beat and breath.

I have a skylark in each ear. Notes candle,
spiral out of hand, and migrate north.

My boots lean into rock and fly peat water.
The mountain runs and stands.

Whimbrel

There is rain and falling night and there is the fjord.
There is the cold north stealing through my coat.
There is a fine dark line drawn through shoreline pebbles.
There is a bird's skull, domed and perfect.
There is its long, curved bill.

There is the shine of iron water and the boggy path.
There is the bird's head snugged in my palm.
There is the white-painted windowsill in the cottage.
There is the bird's skull without memories.
There is night rushing in through its empty eye.

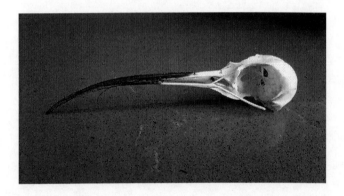

Hekla

still miles from the crater
we lose the tarmac

for two hours we are condemned
to drive on washboard pumice

we see how Hekla is an upturned boat
her cratered keel an offering to north

my pencil skates on the jerking page
of my notebook, I think how

Hekla's centuries rained volcanic ash,
smothered grass outright, sent sheep

bolting in terror, snagged farms in torrents
of lava, shifted whole hillsides in terrible noise

how fish boiled in the rivers and
the mountain's ice was wholly melted

how at times the people observed birds
both large and small, they said,

flying in the mountain's fire
and took them to be souls

Fagradalsfjall

I climbed to the volcano on a bright day, picked my course over plains of scattered pumice, then up an unrelenting steepness, slipping back in ash and gravel. Lungs toiled. I jammed my boots across the gradient. Stopped. Went on. I caught up with the others on a slope littered with rocks. And everyone, friends beside strangers, called out at once because in that minute the volcano rumbled, spat orange fire through smoke that billowed into towers of cloud.

We all heard it roar. We knew what insignificance we'd brought to this place, for all our effort. Alongside people of all nations I stood wondering to watch the tide of lava race downhill as red as blood, as red as meat, lethal, constant, unbridgeable.

And either side of that gory river crackled banks of cooling lava. The valley filled from slope across to slope, the lava spooling greyly into toppled layers, with here and there a vile red eye to wink the thinness of the crust. Heat swarmed up the bank at us. I sidled down to where the mounding lava flared flame-edged. It hissed on the slopes, fired heathers and mosses. It offered us sweet smoke of woodfires, that masked the chemical haze.

I saw a valley's depth devoured in layers of newly-minted stone. Fagradalsfjall that afternoon grew broader with each lava pulse, a magma column towering on gas, unsteady planet's heartbeat. I saw the lava open its raging veins. The valley burned. I witnessed fire flung onto farming land by forces we can't live with.

Translation 1 : magma

molten rock re-forged as glass, stone vitrified white-hot
then shot with air like the bones of birds

stone chilled to rattle in the clouds, falls like rain-
smashed pewter to cool on lower slopes

I pocket a sharp and shining handful from the area
dare touch an alchemy that turns magma into scoria

Vik

Some mornings the van shakes on its wheels
and when I haul the sliding door, the ocean
roars its fury in a voice I've never heard
but feel I might deserve.

Some mornings I walk down to the beach
at Vik. Black sand is soaked to carbon
and the blistered air is stropped with foam.
I pull my hat over my ears.

Some mornings the ocean rumbles like an earthquake
just offshore. I ground my boots in raven sand.
The white comes frothing. Comes sliding up
the beach and I retreat.

Some mornings here it rains salt. Some mornings
the Atlantic flings stones at the beach. Some mornings
are a smashed sea bird and a gull-coloured sea.
Some mornings are hunters.

Glymur and the crossing

We take a path through an arctic edge,
a way of late lupin leaves starred
with rolling beads of mercury.

Our way opens next a narrow stair,
trod into curves by the dryers of cod,
who strung this cave through other years

but stared as we do out through a vast
stone arch, upriver, to where Glymur's
spray grows clouds above the ravine.

Down here the river spools long widths
of cold and we only know the crossing-place
by the steel hawser sunk in each bank.

I take the wire in my hand and there's just
a suggestion of balance, not what
you'd call support, there are tumbled

stepping stones part-submerged,
the water beats and tumbles in my head.
I balance and feel the dare come right.

Midstream pause to duck my body through
below the wire then step onto fifteen feet
of slender log that might carry me to the bank.

Cold water flickers depth and light   I stretch out
my arms above its race and don't look down,
walk the log's road to land   and love, yes love

these steps that will not come again.

Glymur and the whale

The gorge-green cliffs exhilarate
like white-hurtled backs of fulmars.

The little sun draws me a longer
shadow on this stony brink, I

wave to my boots and the vertical drop.
I breathe height above the mossed rocks

down where pale birds call and ledge
through a droplet haze, and fly in constant noise

downstream to the low fjord where once
a faithless man was changed

to a mad red-headed whale. In Faxaflói
he drowned sons and smashed boats

till an old priest spelled his walking stick
and poked it in the sea.

Took water in his shoes, then drew
the whale upriver and shut him

in the wild ravine. The rock walls
clanged with his threshing flukes and

above the old priest limped along the cliffs.
He set the whale like a salmon at the falls.

And all I see is the white birds fly
around his red head.

Translation 2 : troll

inland of the black ash plains and grazing horses
by the long crumpled fields of lava, the trolls

walk in darkness to measure the land, squelch
its names into its floods, turn their arses to its rain

crouched on scarps they lurk the hairy night, and now
and then one fatally mistimes the dawn, stiffens into stone

Power lines

From the moving car I watch these
slow brutes hawsered to an austere land.
I sense their tall integrity, their
criss-cross walk flicks by me,
their ears prick into the rain.

Some poise *en pointe* though most
are braced, all hips and thighs.
They blur the wet car window, frame
after frame of moss and grass, fudged edge
and ridge, all straw and watered grey.

For miles I trace their looping lines through
sky, observe them ankle-deep in scrambled lava,
how roped they are to bedrock.
They scale a land so mutable they shrug off
fallen roads, and the sideslip of old landmarks.

September, and I am being driven in the rain
past the new giants of Iceland, their electric spell.
I will keep listening in fear of the future,
in fear of the stories the pylons will tell.

Dyrhólaey

is licked out by the sea's cold tongue.
The island of the door in the hill
is full of noise, ablaze with daylight.

Fulmars and kittiwakes line ledges,
chatter through white above which
a man might walk the mossed stone

tightrope of the island's lintel,
might watch for seals till dark,
resist the wind from years ago –

the night he followed a sweetness
of singing, walked Reynisfjara beach
to the swaying basalt columns

of the cave and listened, knelt in
a rumple of sealskins on the sand.
How he caught one to his heart

and ran, left the house door swinging
while he stowed the skin in the kist,
dropped the lid and turned the key,

slung it on a thong around his neck.
At daybreak he goes back to find
the woman weeping in the cave.

She knows how this story goes,
walks home with him, loves him, bears
his children down the years until

until one day he hangs his key on the hook
while she trims his hair and he forgets,
forgets and goes down to the fishing –

so at last she hears her smooth and dappled
sealskin sing a tide inside the kist for her.
She uses his key then holds their children,

weeps for their seven children on land,
weeps for her seven children in the sea. She
slithers into her skin and leaves him for the ocean

leaves him on the island of the door in the hill.

Evacuation photographs at Heimaey, 1973
after photographer Kristjan H Kristjansson

The harbour has garnered the red of the night sky,
which is a furnace now. Sea ripples under splashing
floodlights. There is the blur of panic.

January, two in the morning, how the halyards
are clanking on the masts, and that white light crashing
on the decks. The crowd waits on the quay, huddled,

hoods up, shocked from sleep. All their bodies lean
at once towards the boats. Their need to escape is
the biggest thing in the world.

Far too close, a mile-long fissure, deep as a gasp,
roars tongues of flame that silhouette their rooftops.
His head still rings with the hour-ago thunderclap
of the Earth splitting, the dinning of the fire alarms.

He waits to leave, but photographs the island exploding.
He records blasts that shave hill edges in shocks
of sparks. His captured, upflung rocks become
a red murmuration descending on the ordinary.

He frames the fires within the kirkgate arch. His camera
witnesses two crucifixes left to ward off Eldfell.
The boats leave for the mainland, into the dark.

on Wōden's day

we zip east on the ring road
from the back seat I watch

the flat fields stretch towards the dark
there are tatty farms, thin fences, more rain

in a muddy field under Skaftafell
three ravens feed on a lamb

Translation 3 : iceberg

rock-scoring, groaning, clenched to the mother glacier
the bergs are calved at the slow, stained brink

lurch on alone into bitter lake water, savage, salinated
tip up their blue slopes to the low sun, glimmer and wash

down to the beach, shed shattered diamonds on black
satin sand, melt into salt, raise up oceans

The cairns of chance survival
Laufskálavarða

Mile after thin black mile
there's a slab of gritty dark between
the Katla glacier and the sea.

Here have been four parishes of farms
worked and ruined, worked and ruined
by centuries of glacial outburst floods.

A thousand years of hardy horseback farmers
crossed here, forded freezing
racing rivers, slowly rode the lava miles.

In fog and blowing rain, this day, on this endless
plain, where the horses stand waiting, saddled,
thick tails to the grit and silt and ash,

under darkness of rock and sky, the men
are kneeling. They stack one journey's stone up
on the last, for luck, before remounting.

If you are lost

in an Icelandic forest
stand up,

they say, and true, some
trees are only waist-high
thicket and not wood

but tonight these birches
are true forest
they climb the steepness
of sky above us
bend their dark crowns
down on us

we step quick and careful
losing height through
tangled roots that
rib the path
make narrow
staircases that turn
on ruckled landings
light is really going now
we descend descend
the mountain

and at ease, ahead of us
a redwing hops

we leave the glacier
we scramble fast
against the night

within the month
it'll follow us
and migrate south
just now in the near-
dark
it leads the way

Listening in Icelandic

þ

thorn is sharper, distinct at its tip
holds a raindrop pricked onto each
sound that cannot be extended while

ð

eth whispers like its own ghost
trailing a cloud behind it as if you
brushed by softly through the reeds

on the road we passed

a torn tin barn, one rent end
blown out by wind
the other dug deep in the hill

slatted, three-legged shelters
in the fields, where tail-tucked
horses wait out the weather

ground bobbled by ice, its slow
thaw then freeze then thaw
has made *þúfur*, frost-heave

through whose hummocks
more horses pick their way
surefooted, grazing, grazing

acres of rain glisten, and then
flashed through beat of windscreen
wipers, a pink roof, an orange barn

through streaming glass the black ash
miles under Hekla, striated lines
of ridge and furrow, out of scale

although that day we did not pass giants
and we did not pass trolls

Translation 4 : core

where mud is on the boil, thick soup of it belching
brown through streaked yellow, viridian green

and sulphur thick as a cough to clog the throat
while you warm your hands at this frozen hill

which even a mile away was steaming, a boiling cloud
from crevices, from springs, the earth's warm heart

Hestar

They mingle in the fields beside the road
small-statured, muscled to carry a farmer's load
iron grey, mouse grey, and bay

Foals stray from their dams and dance
along a rickety pigwire fence
white-tailed skewbald, wall-eyed piebald

Manes blow back over reins, ground-coverers
all day at *tölt*, sheep-gatherers
copper chestnut, liver chestnut

One horse under saddle, two in hand,
a dorsal stripe, a snip, a blaze
blue roan and brown and yellow dun

A flying stallion at *skeið*, his rider
balanced smooth and still as water
silver-dappled black and dappled grey

Icelandic

the weight over both our heads is Katla
where the glacier's massive shield is
wedged among snowy peaks, impaled
under the sky like a spell on a nail

the mare's mane is brown and falls
coarse on both sides of her neck
grittily her blue hooves sink
into riverbank stone and gravel

she lowers her head to look. I let the reins
run and at once she steps out into the glacial
river. Both her forelegs slide down a hidden
stony shelf and she lunges, with purpose

into the bright water. I follow her sway
with the small of my back
raise up my legs against
her sides, like in the photographs

in the museum, all those farmers raising
their monochrome, gaitered legs
along thick-furred flanks
as their horses waded and splashed

Right now the river covers my mare's knees
and drags at her. The current funnels blue
and fast around her, creates a moment's vertigo
when I can't tell if she's being forced

downstream or if it's just my mind
that's running out to sea

Translation 5 : horse

they rake each other's necks, below the mane
strong yellow teeth at grooming, bonding

staggery foals grow taller, skitter through a year
the best are singled out, but the rest

less strong, less kind, less bold become
peppercorned, an item on the specials menu

Blahnúkúr 1

What I encountered there, I'm still not sure.
We walked in through white tufts
of bog cotton, windbent in the reedy damp.
Bare rock shoulders lifted all around us,
bright as a pencil box. I saw a silver-green
and mauve mountain and thought briefly
of suffragettes, though there was not
a woman on its slopes nor any creature.

Blahnúkúr was like climbing a slagheap. My boots slid
in fine blue grit and the gradient hurt.
I watched slivers of obsidian by the path as I
clambered and I thought of picking one up but knew
not to interrupt the rhythm of breath
and trudge, slow gain of height. When we halted
we sheltered behind a vast obsidian outcrop.
It was blue-black, faceted, shiny.

Below lay the houseless valley, skimmed pale as plaster.
A river coiled. Sharp spurs pitched downwards, lit
with streaks of rhyolite and shadow, a flush
of orange, a blare of lime. Rain flashed across us.
The others climbed on. I waited for the rainbow.
It grew and arched its back. Hidden behind
the rock, I watched it shy like a horse, then fold
its legs, and lay down across the pale gold mountain.

Blahnúkúr 2

The steeps were engraved with zigzags like
a houndstooth carving on a lintel in another country.
I'd have caught my breath but was so short of it.

I stood high just then above a watered geology
of pigments that shifted under my gaze.
Green bled into ochre. Rock was magicked into pool.

The rain swept back, harsher this time. It ran us
down at full gallop and we tore off rucksacks to fumble
for waterproofs, shuddered at sleet on bare skin.

Rain battered on my shoulders, my old coat
leaked and face and fingers stiffened in the cold.
The gilt and silver mountains disappeared.

We knew our limits, retreated off those recent
ancient rocks, turned tail for lower ground.
How brief and small we were beneath that sky.

melt   In High Nowhere now, the glaciers die
they shuck their ancient skins and groan,

shed bergs into a salted lake, a chill blue
wheel of omens dicing in the tide.

We mourn the glaciers. We spell our hearts to cope.
We walk the human path of slightest hope.

FABLE

front   In High Nowhere now, a wind is blowing.
The dry, unripened acorns fall too soon

but tonight fresh rain bends every frond.
Each dangles its bead of light. I lean on the parapet

and such is chance, the river spins me a kingfisher,
a sudden pulsing curve of peacocked flight.

Flown

Then, when I forgot to close my window at night
the room filled up with legs and wings.
I learned to scoop the daddy-long-legs in my palm
so they were tapping hands in my shut fingers
until I soft-pushed them outside again.

Or cupped dusty moths in a beer glass, lidding it
with a postcard. I'd watch the strangeness of their furred
and owlish faces, listen to the panicked whirr of wings.
The silences they left as they flew to twilight.

Now we leave the windows flung wide
in the heated evenings. We leave the lamps lit.
The streets glow. The gardens glow.
And nothing, nothing happens.

40.2 degrees

'Temperatures exceeding 40°C in the UK sounds unfathomable today, but this could become the new norm by the end of the century.'
~ *ZME Science, June 2020*

The day became full of weight. It leaned over and locked us in. A green bloom lay on the garden pond of the unprotected.

First thing, we dragged pots deeper into shade, but later found the heat had scorched leaves anyway.

The sun came too close to us, a slipping forge.

What times are these?

We learned, shut every window, every door. Shut out the light. Indoors, I tasted drought outside.

We put out a thermometer, waited for it to drop to match the heat inside. When evening broke, we threw doors and windows wide into a hot silence. Walked out on the browned grass. Under the still-sweating blue, a dead and desiccated frog.

The Winged Hare

North are tall roofs and chimney pots that do not smoke.
Taller still a Scots pine. My gaze is drawn
to its windy crown and the nest that bristles there.
A pigeon tilts its keel and freewheels down the air.
A bus goes by, and a dog with a man on a lead.

South and the light is going now in garden after garden.
A Wendy house gapes a pink door. A trampoline hoists up
its nets like skirts above the fence. From out of the wind
a winged hare tumbles on my muddied grass.
It crouches. There's some blood. I bend and pick it up.

It weighs more than I thought. Its wings strain leathery
and strong against my coat. *Help me*, it says.
Its voice is iron and berries. And without a further
thought, I heave it high and hurl it into air – where
in a beat it flies, then slants away among the trees.

Clayworm

Work with both hands to soften the clay.
It will be cold as it's dug out of the ground.

Mould it to the writhe of a worm.
If it cracks, damp it in rainwater.

Shape its saddle of eggs and lay
the clayworm out on the ground for a week.

Pray for some warmth.
Pray for the rain to stop.

On the eighth day, wash.
Take up a spade. Dig a grave.

Line its sides with the slates that have fallen
in the empty villages.

Settle the clayworm within the slates.
Cover it lightly with riddled soil.

Now pray it burrows.

The little hedgehog gods

Hibernation would have ended in spring.
So now in February break yeast
into a bowl. Add sugar
with a little warm water.
Mash gently. While you wait

for it to froth, take strong white flour.
Add salt. Then stir the yeast in, with
a little oil. Mix to a soft dough with your fingers.
Look out through your window.

Look for anything green.
Turn out the dough onto a floured table.
Knead it till it's smooth, then
divide it like a root.

Pat and roll the hedgehogs into equal size.
Try not to let there be a runt.
Shape them in your palms, use
scissors to snip their backs to spikes.

Draw out their snouts, and for eyes
press raisins into their heads.
Leave the hedgehogs to rise.
Once grown, brush them

with milk and bake them for ten minutes
until brown. They will ring hollow
under your hand.
Leave them to cool on turned earth.
Consume those that have not left by morning.

Grandmothers

When the grandmothers were let out of prison
they began to darn
for now only the rich could afford new clothes
and everyone else was ragged
or sharing, or buying black market.

The grandmothers darned. They mended cuffs
and necks and elbows. Stitched up holes in pockets.
All winter, they mended even
the fairytales of snow, yes, the snow
that came before the time of rain.

The grandmothers threaded their needles and
told folktales to the children. How you steered
your sledge with your boots, behind you.

The grandmothers snipped their threads and
the children opened their mouths in wonder,
imagining snowflakes falling on their tongues

how cold each one was, and then gone.

PATH

heart   In High Nowhere now red-headed Lords
and Ladies bow their nubbled brows to earth.

Woodpigeons sway first-light their throaty treetops.
The plait of ivy caught round the lime is trembling

with out-of-sight squirrels you'd be sure are full of joy.
In the heart of the wood, I am a walked thought.

Dougie aged eight at Gutcher's Isle

Nothing is accidental here. At the edge
two roofless gables still endure the wind.
The treading sea comes in through granite gates
and keeps a harbour for this steading.

You goat-leap down the slippery path
to where they once drew up a boat.
The slabs rise round us, old as salt.
Their massive stacks bounce back your voice.

Here we crash on mussel shells, look out
to sea through the slapping gate.
You pass me treasures from under our feet –
wet black snailshell, wave of glass.

Above us, thrift heads thatch the granite,
swayed with bees they overlean the sides.
You point to blue sky splashed in white –
a rising sail of butterflies.

Minding the hillfort

Between windfarm and motorway,
Burnswark.

Swallows birl along the steep.
The summit soft with grasses
which fold in the wind
and brush at sky, as I climb.

On the rampart I sit in the wide
world and low sea-dazzle.
Burnswark.

Days later
still a white space
in the head.

Bird Weather

Water-drawn, like so much else,
you cut your engine to long quiet of merse
pick up first distant yammer of the geese.
Starlings blow like passing rain
wet leaves and petrol feathers shine.
A curlew maps the grass-deep lane.

Scots pine, wind-blasted, twisted, holds
the sideslip, dip-glide dark of crows.
You observe sunlit, bentgrass mouseholes.
You know out there is sea, its low roar ceaseless;
know in the mud spring shrilling,
waking northbound geese.

Cerf-volant, two-star municipal, heatwave
Auvergne, June 2022

over the van mirror I
saw him stopped
in the dimming air, held up
on particles of thunder

his antlers curved, a red
and doubled
crescent moon
against a hot and violet sky

he hovered like a hand
wing-cases chittering, raised high
like some dark Gabriel
above the campsite, like

an annunciation so
my skin crawled and I
could not
look away

in Owlpen a spider came out of an egg

her night was yellow and great with the moon
she felt grass grow past her folded legs

when her carapace dried towards dawn
she crept on the earth of Owlpen Wood

all morning she clambered an oak
she was limber and hard to the fresh white sky

she waited for the breath of her god or the planet
she trailed her thread, a hook for the breeze

in Owlpen a spider flew over the land
no-one saw where she went on the wind

no-one heard her set down on a dock
and start spinning her life to the Wolds

her webs tie the lambs to the soil
she'll roll up her life like their wool

build the softest nest for her eggs
and leave us a thread through winter

in Owlpen a spider came out of an egg

path   In High Nowhere now we've no idea
         when seas will rise and night will fall.

         This tender ground is full of paths and graves.
         The dead are always doing something new.

         Meanwhile the living breathe the air. We eat the plants.
         We love. We've work to do.

PS. The cat considers important things

Your concerns on biodiversity, Orlando?

She folds her supple
rasps her tongue down ginger stripes

> *O the skedaddle of dragonflies*
> *when i*
> *haunch-leap claw-snatch all*
> *life-rattle of it in my mouth*
> *i'm never sure if*
> *i'll bite down*
> *or let it go*

Your views on love, Orlando?

> *feed me*

Too early, cat. Wait.

> *rub my ear*
> *the other ear*

> *that's too much*

Your opinion on equality, Orlando?
She is offended, hisses
teeters on
the table edge
slaps with claws extended

> *i'm not afraid of you*
> *and*
> *nobody picks me up*

And what about the climate crisis, Orlando?

> *your problem*

Notes

1937, Tasmanian Tiger

The word 'endling' was coined for the last Tasmanian Tiger, or Thylacine, who died in Hobart Zoo in 1937. She was referred to as Benjamin, despite being female. In the 21st century US artist Thylobscene makes aboriginal-inspired art of the thylacine, based on cave paintings.

Yewei

Yewei: 'wild taste'
This poem is based on an essay by Jane Qiu, published in National Geographic in July 2022.

A wish on the Glynch

This sequence of poems was written at Clenchers Mill in Herefordshire during the time I was Troubadour of the Hills for Ledbury Poetry Festival and Malvern Hills AONB. The flour dresser machine, a mechanised early flour sieve, was also known as the 'bolter', and it does indeed make a loud sound like galloping hooves.

Two Stroke, from 1919

I was shown a small two stroke agricultural engine during my time as poet in residence at Acton Scott Historic Working Farm Museum. These little engines transformed the drudgery of farm labouring work in the 1920s.

Translation 1: magma

Scoria forms when magma containing abundant dissolved gas flows from a volcano or is blown out during an eruption. As the molten rock emerges from the earth, the pressure upon it is reduced and the dissolved gas starts to escape in the form of bubbles, causing cavities in the rock. This dark-coloured igneous rock with the trapped bubbles is known as scoria.

Glymur and the whale

The huge waterfall at Glymur is linked to a folktale in which the community is menaced by an angry, red-headed whale. The local priest charms the creature into the gorge and up the falls. The whale dies at last in Hvalvatn, the lake above the waterfall – where, eerily, whalebones have been discovered.

Dyrhólaey

Dyrhólaey translates as 'the island of the door in the hill'. The selkie tale is specific to Reynisfjara beach.

Evacuation photographs at Heimaey, 1973

The young Kristjan H Kristjansson was evacuated with his parents, and all the inhabitants of the island of Heimaey, on 23 January 1974. He was a keen photographer, and recorded the events of that night. The fissure eruption later developed into a single active crater in the middle of the rift, named Eldfell, or Fire Mountain. He writes that some of his photographs of that night are blurred, as he forgot his tripod in the hurry. You can find his photographs on YouTube.

Listening in Icelandic

Thorn þ and eth ð are still found in Icelandic, with their origins in old Norse, old English and others. Both give a "th" sound, but thorn is voiced, like the sound in 'the', while eth is its unvoiced counterpart, like the sound at the end of 'with'.

On the road we passed

þúfur – also written thúfur – are cold climate landforms which appear in regions of permafrost and seasonally frozen ground.

Hestar

Hestar (Icelandic) – horses
There are over forty colours and variations amongst Icelandic horses.
Tölt and skeið are the extra gaits of the Icelandic horse.

Blahnúkúr

Translates as 'blue mountain', an extinct volcano formed of dust and lava, with black obsidian erratics – in contrast with the brightly coloured Rhyolite mountains on the other side of the Landmannalaugar valley.

Dougie aged eight at Gutcher's Isle

The isolated ruins of a 17th century farmstead overlooking Gutcher's Isle on the Solway coast no doubt played their part in the smuggling trade during the 18th century. 'A poor Man named Gutcher, lived in a temporary Shed on this Island for some time hence its name.' *Ordnance Survey Name Book, Kirkcudbrightshire 1848-51*

Bird Weather

Written at Mersehead Nature Reserve on the northern shore of the Solway. Huge numbers of Barnacle geese overwinter there before leaving in April for Greenland and Svalbard.

Thanks and Acknowledgements

Poems in this collection were first published in Raceme, Anthropocene, Write Where We Are Now, Poetry Scotland, Columba, One Hand Clapping, Finished Creatures, Interpreter's House, The Lake, ARTEMISpoetry, Pennine Platform and Poetry Wales.

I am so grateful to Steve Griffiths for his constant encouragement and patient reading of the manuscript. This is a better book because of him. Huge thanks to Þrúður Helgadóttir and Joe Greatorex for showing me Iceland, answering constant questions and bearing with my attempts to grasp something of the language. And to members of Border Poets, who have been hugely supportive to me over the years, maintaining my confidence in my work alongside proper, serious criticism – my thanks. My love and thanks as ever to Paul, Lenny and Dougie, who remain supportive, inventive and hopeful. I owe Lenny in particular for his thoughts on viruses. Orlando was no help at all.

Previous Publications:

The Bicycles of Ice and Salt, 2021, IDP.
Fan-peckled, 2021, Fair Acre Press.
Understories, 2019, Whalebone Music.
How Time is in Fields, 2019, IDP.
Luck's Weight, 2014, Biscuit Tin Press.
The Henkeeper's Almanac, 2013, Biscuit Tin Press.
Not Lost Since Last Time, 2013, Oversteps Books.
The Dark Farms, 2011, Roncadora Press.
Lost at Sea, 2010, Roncadora Press.

Indigo Dreams Publishing Ltd
24, Forest Houses
Cookworthy Moor
Halwill
Beaworthy
Devon
EX21 5UU
www.indigodreamspublishing.com